Little Venice, L(

An Illustrated Guide

Robert Tyler

Worth Publishing

www.worthpublishing.com

Little Venice, London
An Illustrated Guide

Written and photographed by
Robert Tyler

Published by Worth Publishing Ltd, 2000

This book is sold subject to the condition that it shall not, by way of trade or otherwise, be lent, re-sold, hired out or otherwise circulated without the publisher's consent in any form of binding or cover other than that in which it is published and without a similar condition being imposed on the subsequent purchaser.

© Robert Tyler 2000

First published in Great Britain in 2000 by Worth Publishing Ltd
Lauderdale Parade, London W9 1LU

ISBN 1-903269-01-6

Typeset by Digital Reproductions Ltd, Huntingdon, Cambs

Printed and bound in Great Britain by the Bath Press Limited, Bath

All rights reserved. No part of this publication may be reproduced, stored in a retrieval system, or transmitted in any form, or by any means, electronic, mechanical, photocopying, recording or otherwise, without the prior permission of the publishers.

Little Venice, London

To the Bun

Acknowledgements

Completing a book is always a team effort and this is no exception.

I should particularly like to thank Rohan Acharya of the Canal Café Theatre, Beryl Kendall of the English Watercolour Gallery, Alex Prowse, Grenville Middleton of the puppet theatre, Dennis Moore, David Snowdon and the Irish Georgian Society, all of whom provided valuable insights into the area and its people. I should also like thank all the managers and proprietors of the various establishments mentioned within the book for their help in preparing useful information. The staff at Marylebone Library, Westminster Reference Library, the Westminster City Archives, British Waterways, the London Transport Museum and the London Canal Museum were, as always, courteous and helpful.

Finally I am deeply indebted to Laura Morgan of Worth Publishing, whose tireless search for authenticity and accuracy in the detail presented and whose skill and trained eye for design and layout has created such a fine finished product.

Robert Tyler, Little Venice, August 2000

Maps on page 19 and 39 reproduced by permission of the City of Westminster Archives Centre. Poster on page 22 reproduced by permission of the London Transport Museum. Puppet postcards on page 62 reproduced by kind permission of Grenville Middleton. Quotations from *The Short Stories of Katherine Mansfield* on pages 51 and 52 reproduced by kind permission of Alfred A. Knopf, a division of Random House Inc. Photograph on page 66 reproduced by permission of the Freud Museum, London. Quotation from *Grasshopper* by Barabara Vine on page 80 © 2000 by Kingsmarkham Enterprises. Reprinted by permission of Penguin Books Canada Limited, Penguin Books Limited and the Peters Fraser and Dunlop Group Limited.

Little Venice, London

Contents

Introduction	2
The Origins of Little Venice	6
The Coming of the Canals	8
Architecture and Style	24
House and Street Life in Little Venice	36
The People who Lived in Little Venice	44
Leisure and Pleasure	56
How to Get Here	82
Index	85

Little Venice, London

Venice. Hot and humid. Misty light filtering through lazy canals. Crumbling shadows in the canal water reflecting palladian architecture as the Gondoliero glides you by. Unexpected quiet as a canal corner is turned leading to further echoing streets and water byways. As dusk falls ever more people gather in waterside restaurants lit only by candles and their own glistening suntan.

Little Venice, London provides much Venetian atmosphere and joie de vivre but remarkably in a space about a fiftieth of the size of the real Venice. Its canals were constructed three hundred years later but for the same commercial purpose - transport. The area boasts the hottest temperatures in the UK, there really is a Gondola (sadly beached on a barge), the streets reflect a graceful stucco architecture both light and beautiful and the popular cafés and restaurants are enlivened by the glowing faces of the cosmopolitan clientele.

Little Venice, London

The Lido, Venice

Little Venice, London

2

Little Venice is a place that people think they have heard of but can't quite place on the map of London. In its brief history this part of Maida Vale has not always been as highly sought after as it is now. Unpromisingly occupying an area to the west of the Edgware Road and north of the A40 (just before it hits the traffic lights of Euston Road), the entire district was built between 1810 and 1870 and was the haunt of artists, writers, prostitutes, scientists and London commuters. The second oldest profession has now moved to other pastures but today's occupants are a polyglot and diversely talented community enjoying a quiet proximity to the bustling life of London's West End, a mere mile to the south.

The essential joy and charm of Little Venice lies in its canal waterway base and in the white stucco five- and six-storey houses that border its broad tree-lined streets.

This book draws together Little Venice's past and present and offers residents and visitors a pictorial memory, a short history and a description of today's delights within one of London's best kept secrets. Amongst the canals and stucco buildings the famous and sometimes infamous have flourished or languished and the better known are included in the book which, for reasons of privacy and taste, declines to disclose details of those residents (including the author) who are still alive and very much kicking.

Although ownership of theatres, pubs and restaurants inevitably changes over time, justice to Little Venice would not be done without a comprehensive inclusion of these as they currently are, since they contribute so much to the spirit and buzz of the area. Many photographs have been included not because the author is a better photographer than writer, but principally to show the calm beauty of the architecture and the reflective wash of the canal waters that makes Little Venice so unique.

Little Venice, London

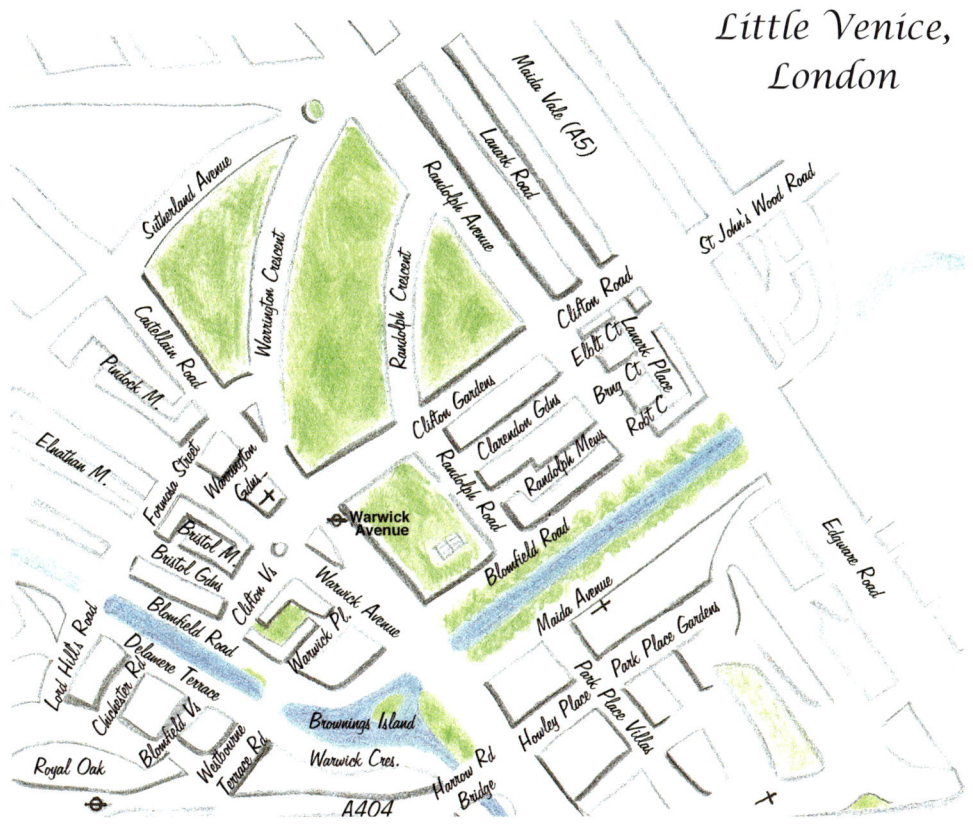

The Origins of Little Venice

The abbots of West Minster were granted most of West London by charter in 1222 when it was farmland. Naturally Henry VIII rode roughshod over this arrangement, but shortly after his death in 1547 the area was handed back to the Bishops of London. Over the next two hundred years the Bishops granted farm leases until the arrival in the second half of the eighteenth century of the canal building companies. In 1796 land for canal construction was sold to the Grand Junction Canal Company by an Act of Parliament. In 1836 the Ecclesiastical Commissioners took over from the Bishops and some surplus land was sold off. From then Parliament allowed ground leases to be granted by the church to enable the expanding population of West London to own and build houses.

In the seventeenth century, however, the Bishops leased about a third of their holding to the Frederick family, one of whom was Lord Mayor of London. A direct descendant, Robert Thistlethwaite, inherited most of what is now Little Venice from the Fredericks. But where, specifically, is the area known as "Little Venice"? The map on page 5 is as close a definition as exists. The Roman Edgware Road (the A5 which travels straight to North Wales) forms the eastern boundary to Little Venice. The construction of the Grand Union canal formed the western boundary. The northern boundary is effectively where the stucco buildings peter out at the Warrington Hotel, and the southern boundary is formed by the canalside street Maida Avenue, together with Park Place Villas and Howley Place.

The Origins of Little Venice

The Coming of the Canals

Barges, Grand Union Canal

The Coming of the Canals and the Birth of Little Venice

Canal waterways brought unprecedented prosperity to the areas they bisected. The peak period of canal construction and usage was between the years 1760-1850. During that period 2,500 miles of canal were completed in order to link the main industrial and population centres in England and Wales.

The brick or stone encased water ducts provided their huge floating metal barges with slow bulk carrying routes throughout England and a conduit for import and export business. Heavy goods, such as building materials - stone, brick, timber, lime, cement, tiles and slate; also barrels and crates for storage - were transported, in the main, from the North to London, whilst refuse from the City of London was returned and used as fuel for kilns on the brickfields.

However, coal for the new Gas Station constructed in 1823 at King's Cross and Haggerston (near Islington) represented half of all tonnage carried on the barges in the Little Venice area.

The barges were drawn by horses and operated by the itinerant bargee and his family. Once the goods carried by the barges arrived they were loaded onto horse-driven carts for delivery to shops and factory warehouses. Feed for the horses was also brought by canal, and horse manure returned to the country as fertiliser.

There were two types of craft on the canals. Barges, which were four metres wide - a few examples remain alongside Blomfield Road - and narrow boats; two metres wide, faster and used for passenger travel. From the 1830s onwards the bargee and his family also lived on the boat. Such was the grime and dirt created by the cargo and later by steam driven craft that the families took to painting their boat as a way of invoking the bright colours of the countryside for which they yearned. This tradition survives today, and brightly painted private craft adorn the canalsides and provide the romantic colour that makes Little Venice such a delight. The 'Tarporley', bought by the Grand Union Canal in 1937, was a working narrow boat with boatman's cabin and has been preserved by Camden Council. It can now be visited at the Little Venice basin.

The Coming of the Canals

The Coming of the Canals

The development of the canal system within Little Venice was linked to the creation of the Grand Junction Canal on which excavation started in 1793. The Grand Junction Canal was London's link to the industrial areas around Birmingham in the Midlands, 100 miles north-west of Little Venice. The purpose was to link up to the river Thames to enable import and export directly to and from the industrial heartland.

In 1805 the Grand Junction had been completed, entering the Thames at Brentford in West London. In 1794 the Canal Company had also decided to construct a canal link with a major new road which connected Paddington to the City of London, by constructing the Paddington Arm (known as the Paddington branch of the Grand Union Canal today). Entering the Little Venice pool from the north west the canal terminates at Paddington basin at the eastern end of Praed Street with a four hundred yard long wharf where warehouses and pens for livestock were built. The Paddington Canal was finally completed in 1801 and was an instant success as a food distribution point for central London. Celebrations are bound to be taking place to commemorate its 200th anniversary in 2001.

Canals were also immediately used as passenger transport - a service still performed today. The trip to Uxbridge from Paddington was popular and the man who ran it, Thomas Homer, was later to be the instigator of the other canal link at Little Venice pool; the Regent Canal named after the Prince Regent, who was to become King George IV.

The Regent's Canal Act of 1812 authorised the construction of the link from Paddington through Regent's Park and Camden to Limehouse in East London where the waterway would link up with the Thames. The London Canal Museum, opened by the Princess Royal in 1992, lies on this canal stretch off Wharf Road in King's Cross.

Thomas Homer (who was later deported for embezzlement of canal funds whilst Treasurer of the Regent Canal Company) approached the great Regency architect John Nash (who was designing the formal buildings and terraces that now grace Regent's Park) for permission to run the canal through the Park. This was granted, but Nash stipulated that it be sunk below eye level on the northern boundary of the park. Construction eventually started on the huge tunnel a quarter of a kilometre long running eastwards under the Edgware Road to complete the Regent's Canal. The earth excavated was deposited on land belonging to Thomas Lord and now forms the foundations of Lord's Cricket Ground.

The Coming of the Canals

Once completed the only method of moving the barge through the tunnel was for the bargee to lie on his back on top of the barge and use his legs to push on the tunnel roof - the origin of the phrase 'legging it'. After endless problems with existing landowners, workers, engineering difficulties with canal lock devices and lack of funding (not least thanks to Homer), the whole project was finally completed in 1820 and the Little Venice pool at Warwick Crescent took shape as a canal junction point.

Canal barges were horse drawn and today there are still examples of 'horse gullies' leading from the towpath (the name derives from towing barges) into the canal. Horses frequently fell into the water and they had to be towed along in the canal until a gully appeared and they could be drawn up the slope. In the heat of summer the horses would simply be let back down the gully into the water to cool off.

Although the new canal carried 195,000 tons of cargo in its first year of operation - and over 1 million tons in 1829 - it eventually declined in commercial importance (as did all other canals) with the success of the new railway network from 1840. It found lasting success, however, providing pleasure tours and 'country excursions'. The trip from Little Venice to Camden market, the most attractive short stretch to experience, is still highly popular today (of which more later).

The canal operators obtained income from canalside tolls strategically placed throughout the national network. Charges were based on the amount and type of cargo carried. The Regent Canal Toll House beneath the Warwick Avenue Bridge was constructed in 1820 for this purpose. Another toll house for the Paddington Canal, under the Westbourne Terrace Road Bridge, is now operated by British Waterways as an office dedicated to the care and preservation of Britain's canal network.

Toll House, Westbourne Terrace Road Bridge

The Coming of the Canals

During the Napoleonic Wars in the early nineteenth century canal workers supported the crown in its endeavours to defeat Napoleonic aggrandisement and the canals themselves were used for military purposes. By 1825, only eight years after the Napoleonic wars were over, the canal workforce was far from quiescent, demanding higher wages and threatening industrial action on many occasions. The 'leggers' were reportedly a particularly rowdy bunch and in 1826 attempts were made to replace them with steam-engined barges.

Originally canal barge owners were merchants with a house and family in the country. From 1840 onwards, however, as the railways overtook canals as the providers of bulk commercial transport, life got tougher for these families and in one generation they went from comfortable professional class to uncomfortable working class. Inessential crew members were dismissed and the whole family joined the bargee, often closeted in a tiny room in part of the working barge.

With the establishment in 1837 of the Birmingham to London railway terminating at Euston, and of the Great Western Railway terminating at Paddington, the canals were doomed to extinction as economic enterprises, although amazingly some canals were still being used in a small way commercially as late as the 1950s.

The Grand Junction Canal Company purchased the Grand Union Canal in 1894. In 1929 the Grand Junction Canal linked with the Regent's Canal together with various canals in the Midlands to form the Grand Union Canal, by which name the entire network in Little Venice is now known.

The tree planting in the small island in the middle of Little Venice pool, attractively lit at night, known as 'Browning's Island', is reputed to have been requested by Robert Browning (see later) when he lived on the edge of the pool in Warwick Crescent during the years 1862-1887.

'Browning's Island'

The Coming of the Canals

A map of the area in 1810 shows it to be farmland only, but from 1825 construction began on homes for the more affluent in Maida Avenue (then known as Maida Hill West), south of the Regent's Canal, which had been completed by 1834. The Regent's Canal engineer, William Jessop, realised that because the canal had to be cut deep into the slight rise at Maida Hill the houses along the canal edge at Maida Avenue could be sold at higher ground rents, since their view would be uninterrupted. Consequently by 1840 a few substantial and elegant houses in Park Place, Howley Place and three in Warwick Avenue south of the Regent's Canal had been built.

By 1850 Westbourne Terrace Road, Blomfield Road, Mews and Villas, Clifton Villas, Warwick Avenue and the canal end of Portsdown Road (now Randolph Avenue) were constructed. By 1865 most of the roads which make up Little Venice had been completed - Warwick Crescent, Bristol Gardens and Delamere Terrace in the 1850s; Formosa Street, Randolph Crescent, Randolph Avenue, Clarendon Gardens and Clifton Gardens in the 1860s.

The Coming of the Canals

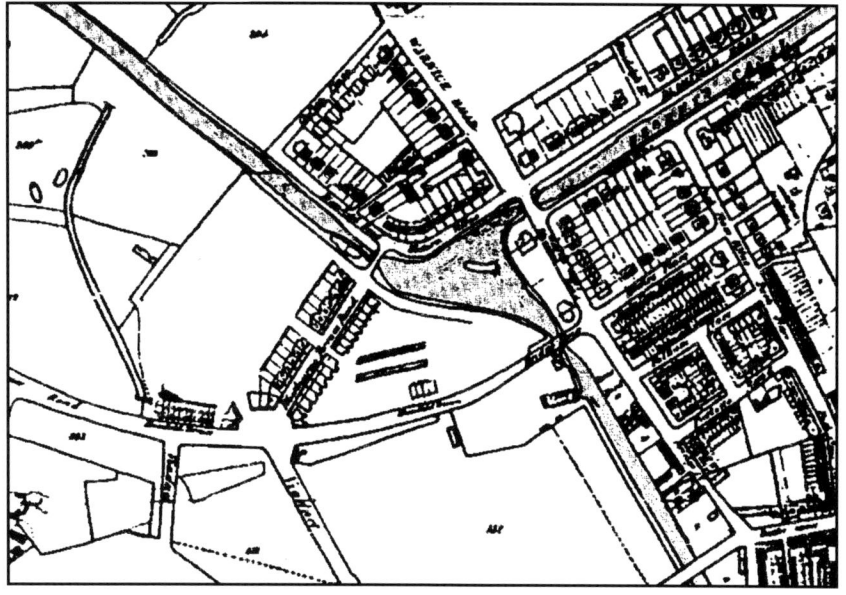

Map of 1849

The Coming of the Canals

Considering that the whole area had been quiet farmland at the turn of the century, this was a real flurry of building activity. Many of the semi-detached houses were substantial but shabbily built, and the white stucco finish so characteristic of this and a few other London districts nicely hid the brick and stone imperfections. Many of the early inhabitants lived on the barges that were moored in profusion canalside. The early houses were occupied initially by the professional classes.

The coming of the Steam railways from 1837 - the year Great Western Railways was formed, ironically based just half a kilometre away at Paddington station - led to the gradual decline of the canal waterway as the main commercial transport and with it, temporarily, the interest in living in the canalside area. However, in 1881 W. S. Clark published *Suburban Homes of London*. In it he says of Little Venice '...roads, crescents, terraces...the degraded forms and habits formerly prevalent have been made to give place to culture, piety and comfort'. The area was on the up, and has not looked back since.

A comparison to the real Venice was possibly first used for the area around the time (1889) of the death in Venice of a famous former resident, the poet Robert Browning. Ruskin and Lord Byron also have claims on first usage, Byron having said, somewhat generously, '...there would be nothing to make the canal of Venice more than that of Paddington, were it not for its artificial adjuncts.' The name Little Venice, however, does not appear to have been in common use until after the Second World War ended in 1945.

The Coming of the Canals

Commercial canal transport continued until the 1950s. The style and history of canal life is celebrated once a year by a festival in Little Venice pool on the first weekend in May. Today's barge owners and operators gather together in the Little Venice Pool, each in their individual barge. Considerable skill and co-operation is needed to get thirty or forty barges into the confined space of the pool. The former canal age of hard physical work for often little reward produced a strong sense of fellowship and community that is reflected at this event. Organised by the Inland Waterways Association, a body dedicated to preserving and promoting the canal network, it makes a stunningly colourful sight for those lucky enough to be there. The illuminated craft and sizzling barbecues maintain the party atmosphere well into the night. On Monday, relaxed and satisfied, the barge operators drift back home, often over 100 miles north.

"IWA Canalway Cavalcade", May Bank Holiday, Little Venice Pool

Architecture and Style

Clifton Gardens

The Architecture and Style of Little Venice Buildings

One of the joys of living in Little Venice is the sight of the early morning sunlight in spring or early summer catching the top floors of the white stucco terraced houses that line the main roads and crescents. The London plane trees that border the wide streets make a soft light filter, casting gentle shadows on the first floor balconies. The banks of white houses are reminiscent of Mediterranean seaside villas - a perfect background for colourful flowers and exotic garden plants.

The essential building style is Regency, the eclectic style associated with the Regency in 1811-20 of the then Prince of Wales George Augustus, later George IV. As a style it is

Architecture and Style

refreshingly light and exuberant yet classical in form and proportion. Its freshness comes from the stucco art style, the white plaster wash that covers all the main buildings in the area. As a result many people still regard the Regency style as the most beautiful in recent architectural history. The architects of Little Venice filched the best ideas from the rococo and neo-classical styles prevalent in the previous century.

Rococo (from the French word rocaille meaning rock-work) was an art style of the eighteenth century characterised in buildings by elaborate ornamentation based on arabesques (flowing sculptured lines often based on foliage), shells, urns and elaborate abstract curves. Many of these features appear in Little Venice, in the magnificent villas at the Warwick Avenue end of Maida Avenue and in Randolph Road for example.

Architecture and Style

The neo-classicists emerged after original Roman and Greek buildings were unearthed by excavation at Pompeii, Italy in 1748 and Herculaneum, Greece in 1738. The porticoes and some window architraves in many of the streets in Little Venice reflect these traditions. The high ceilings, particularly on first and second floors in many of the houses, very much restate classical lines and proportions. Ceilings are typically 12 feet high, corniced and often with floor to ceiling large pane windows. Not surprisingly, therefore, streets and individual houses are still called 'villas' (Park Place, Clifton, Blomfield).

Classical Villa, Warwick Avenue

But the crowning glory is surely the white stucco finish. Stucco, though an Italian word, has an old German derivation meaning 'crust' - an appropriate term for the plaster that covers virtually every frontage in the area. Stucco is composed of gypsum, marble dust and glue. Gypsum, which is mined in England, is hydrous sulphate of lime that becomes plaster of Paris when the water content is heated off. Stucco was used by both Greek and Roman builders for frescoes. Stuccowork reached its peak in the form of twisted columns and carved figures in the 17th and 18th centuries.

Architecture and Style

In England the architect Robert Adam used it extensively for ceiling and wall decorations and friezes. In Little Venice stucco is used in the small bust of the thirteenth century Italian religious artist, Giotto, over the porch at the side of 25, Blomfield Road, in the delicate face carvings in Warwick Avenue villas, in porticoes, in ionic columns, in window architrave features and pretty well everywhere else externally! Stucco finish requires frequent renewal, particularly after prolonged rainfall, a fact that may explain the presence of scaffolding over many houses in the area throughout the year.

Giotto

The final touch to the houses and villas once built was the addition of first floor balconies and ground floor palisades and security railings. The balconies of Little Venice are a distinctive feature and many today sport miniature gardens. The safety railings around the balcony, usually constructed over the

Architecture and Style

main entrance porch, are either made of stone or iron - the majority are elaborately worked cast iron, although some of the Blomfield Road railings are wrought iron.

Cast iron was used in Europe for ornamental work from the early nineteenth century. Since much of Little Venice was constructed between 1840 and 1870 the designers were able to draw on a new artistic influence - the Arts and Crafts Movement - from 1850. The Little Venice architects reverted back to wrought iron, the traditional and intricate skill of the village blacksmith, at a time

when the Arts and Crafts Movement and its famous promoter, William Morris, were praising the value and satisfaction of 'home-made' produce. The majority of the original wrought ironwork of Little Venice appears, however, to have been progressively replaced by cast iron. Although iron casting is a production process involving stamping and extruding rather than a blacksmith's forge, the final result is similar.

Architecture and Style

The Warwick Avenue Canal Bridge railings are typical examples of cast iron work looking as intricate as wrought iron.

Warwick Avenue Canal Bridge

The wide, round-railed balconies on many of the houses are thought to have been so designed to allow twirling distance for Victorian ladies and their crinolines in order to preserve essential decorum!

Architecture and Style

The combination of black railings and white facia on so many properties has prompted an informal agreement amongst present day house owners to prefer black front doors - a rule particularly well observed in Blomfield Road.

Today, the elegant and beautiful backdrop of white faced building and delicate railing enhances the colour of the flowers and skilfully sited potted plants in the formal front gardens of many of the houses. The mild climate and generally low wind levels have also encouraged the growth of palm trees and other sub-tropical plants. One of London's best garden centres, Clifton Nurseries in Clifton Villas, supplies these natural final touches, contributing greatly to the area's outstanding attractions.

Clifton Nurseries, Clifton Villas

Architecture and Style

Unusual Buildings

In 1820 the Grand Junction Canal company constructed a toll house at the narrowest point at the junction of the Regent Canal with the Grand Union at the Warwick Avenue bridge (now called Junction House) and also one for the northerly reach of the Junction canal under the Westbourne Terrace Road bridge. These toll houses were always strategically positioned and exacted payment from the passing barge operator on the basis of the type of cargo and the weight being carried, the weight being estimated by the level of the barge in the water. This was the sole source of income at this time for the canal companies, the barges being owned by the businesses using them. In the twentieth century some canal companies bought barges and hired them out to users. The building under the Westbourne Terrace Road bridge is used an office for the London Region of British Waterways where details can be obtained on the canals and also licences issued for canal use such as canoeing - a popular pastime on the canal.

Junction House

Warwick Avenue
Teahouse

In the centre of Warwick Avenue lies a recently restored Victorian wooden teahouse exclusively reserved for London taxi drivers. These green wooden huts - of which there are now thirteen throughout central London - were instituted by the philanthropist 7th Earl of Shaftesbury in the 1870s and are run by the Cabmen's Shelter Fund. Each hut has a name; this one is simply called Warwick Avenue. The idea was originally sponsored by a group of the landed gentry eager to sober up drunken cabbies with warm tea and cake and thus maintain a safe service. The hut area also provides a place to park up - particularly welcome on a damp foggy winter's evening. Although officially reserved for licensed London taxi drivers, currently numbering around 22,000, a persuasive passer-by might get a cup of tea for twenty-five pence!

Architecture and Style

The blue and gold painted canal bridges in Little Venice were constructed in the 1890s.

Stone pineapples are a strong feature on various houses, particularly in Formosa Street. The pineapple is a traditional symbol of hospitality and welcome and is also prominent all along the East Coast of the USA. In the 1860s in Little Venice, as elsewhere in England, pineapples were a new and exotic imported fruit and must have represented a touch of architectural one upmanship for the house owner of which Stephen Potter (of whom more later) would have been proud.

Architecture and Style

House and Street Life in Little Venice

House and Street Life in Little Venice

Most of the Regency properties have a basement and four or five floors above. The most attractive rooms were originally first floor drawing rooms. Most of the terraced houses and many of the villas have been divided into flats, usually one per floor. First floor tends to be the most desirable because of the balcony and the ceiling height of the rooms, but garden flats are also popular. Many of the streets form private garden squares or triangles behind and one boasts a tennis court.

Private gardens in Little Venice

In 1918, at the end of the First World War, a large bomb reduced part of Warrington Crescent to rubble. During the Second World War Paddington station was a natural target for German bombers and, according to a bomb damage map of 1953, Clifton Gardens at numbers 40 plus was devastated, as was most of the area between Blomfield Road and Clifton Road.

Lanark Road also suffered at its western junction with Sutherland Avenue, but most other areas in Little Venice escaped. Thus here and there the original buildings are either propped up with 1950s council built property as part of an essential rehabilitation for the people of the area, or have been redeveloped as small private housing mews.

In 1889 Charles Booth, a wealthy businessman, undertook a study of the wealth of the residents of Little Venice (and London in general). An early exponent of socio-demographics, Booth produced a fascinating guide to the affluence of the local population. He divided the people of Little Venice by social class, from very poor to wealthy, the results of which he used to produce his famous Poverty Map of 1889 ('wealthy' meant having three or more servants). He concluded at the time that 70% of Londoners lived 'in comfort'; a conclusion not to be taken too seriously given that Booth was out to prove that London's poor was not the political problem described by the radical politicians of the day. In Little Venice most of the area is labelled 'well-to-do', meaning at least one servant, although Bristol Gardens and Formosa Street appear a little lower on the scale, honoured by the dubious distinction of possessing 'working class comfort'.

Today most of the residents would probably accept a description of 'living in comfort'. Although most property is in private hands now the Church Commissioners still own a number of properties in Little Venice.

Booth's Poverty Map 1889

■ Lowest Class. Vicious, semi-criminal.
■ Very poor, casual. Chronic want.
■ Poor. 18s to 21s a week for moderate family.
■ Mixed. Some comfortable, others poor.
■ Fairly comfortable. Good, ordinary earnings.
■ Middle class. Well-to-do.
■ Upper-middle and upper classes. Wealthy.

How the Streets Were Named

Robert Thistlethwaite, who had inherited most of Little Venice from the Fredericks family, also owned lands outside London. His wife's family estate was Clarendon Park in Wiltshire.

Her sister was married to Sir John Morehead who was father-in-law to Jane Warwick of Warwick Hall in Cumbria. This explains the origin of Warwick Avenue and Crescent and Clarendon Gardens.

There were two Bishops of London, Blomfield and Randolph, after whom the streets were named. Randolph Avenue was named as late as 1939, having previously been Portsdown Road, notwithstanding the 'randy' associations (see below)!

Formosa Street

The name 'Formosa' was given to the street off Warrington Crescent following a visit to the island of Formosa itself (now Taiwan) by a member of the Young family of Cookham in Berkshire, who had served as a naval commander in the Far East. This family had links with the Praed family (there is Praed Street in Paddington) who were investors in the canal company that bought land in the vicinity.

The origins of other street names are not so clear. It is probable that the birth of the Great Western Railway in 1837 operating trains to the West Country of England, in particular Bristol, of which Clifton was and still is a smart district, gave rise to Clifton Gardens and Bristol Gardens.

Little is known about the derivation of Lanark Road, Portsdown Road (now Randolph Avenue) or Warrington Crescent.

Street Character

The finest houses are the huge Regency semi-detached buildings, which were first built in the area in the 1840s at Park Place, and then later at Blomfield Road immediately bordering the Regent's Canal. Clarendon Gardens is the most perfectly preserved street, with ionic porticoes and iron balconies spanning the full length of the road on both sides. Randolph Road, Randolph Crescent and the early numbers of Randolph Avenue are also very well preserved. Clifton Gardens sustained some bomb damage in the last war but is wide and lined with trees.

Clarendon Gardens

House and Street Life in Little Venice

The sweep of Warrington Crescent is curvaceously attractive and leads to Formosa Street, which is preserved partially as a shopping street with one pub. The other shopping streets are Clifton Road off Clifton Gardens, the north side of which is original nineteenth century, Warwick Place and Bristol Gardens. Bristol Gardens is a charming and discreet small street with one hotel and some ground floor offices along the eastern side. In the early twentieth century it was a shopping street with a carpet shop, greengrocer and barber.

The natural centre of the area is Warwick Avenue, the widest thoroughfare, and the underground tube station there is an ideal kicking off point for walkers keen to explore the whole district.

Blomfield Road

The Randolph Road area developed a 'character' all of its own from 1880. Rich businessmen used the houses in the area to ensconce their mistresses, a practice that continued as late as the 1950s, when the area was widely known as a high-class red light district. Such was the reputation of the area that the word 'randy' originates in the conduct of Randolph Road's illustrious residents.

Little Venice has hotels, pubs, theatres, art galleries, churches and many cafés/restaurants which are described later in the book. Today the streets are restful, making a Sunday afternoon stroll a delight.

The People

The People Who Lived in Little Venice

The Blue Plaque on a house wall is Britain's way of commemorating the great and the good of the past. Little Venice has 5 such plaques:

    Sir Ambrose Fleming   *(Clifton Gardens)*
    David Ben Gurion   *(Warrington Crescent)*
    Andreas Kalvos   *(Sutherland Avenue)*
    Arthur Lowe   *(Maida Avenue)*
    Alan Turing   *(Warrington Crescent)*

and a truly fascinating group they are.

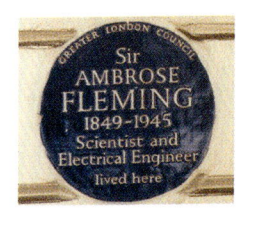

Sir John Ambrose Fleming (1849-1945) lived at 9, Clifton Gardens. He was the inventor of the vacuum-tube diode, now replaced by the transistor. Diodes are used extensively in the rectification of alternating current[1]. Fleming worked closely with

---

[1] Rectification in electricity is the process of converting alternating current (AC) which flows back and forth in a circuit to direct current (DC) which flows only in one direction. Fleming's invention created a device known as a rectifier, which permits flow in one direction, blocking out the other direction, and is inserted in to the circuit for

Logie Baird, Edison and Marconi in the development of the radio, TV and electric lighting. He was a professor at University College, London for 41 years.

David Ben Gurion (1886-1973) was the first Prime Minister of Israel. Born in Russia, he became committed to Zionism (the movement to settle and unite Jews in Palestine). Ben Gurion saw Zionism as a practical idea for Jewish immigration to Palestine and for building the land through collective labour. He moved to Palestine in 1906 where he began organising workers into Unions.

He obtained a law degree from the University of Constantinople in 1914. He was expelled from Palestine in 1915 by the Ottoman Empire authorities and went to the US. In 1917 Britain issued the Balfour Declaration expressing government support for the establishment of a Jewish homeland in Palestine. Ben Gurion joined the Jewish Legion - a voluntary military organisation formed to assist British troops in liberating Palestine from Ottoman rule.

---

this purpose. Among the uses for rectification are the detection of AM radio signals and the operation of heavy electrical machinery, demonstrating the importance of Fleming's invention.

The People

In 1922 the League of Nations issued a mandate granting the British Government control over Palestine. Ben Gurion founded the Mapai (Israel Workers Party) in 1930. From 1935-1948 he was chairman of the Jewish Agency for Palestine and, living in London at Warrington Crescent, advised the British about the establishment of a Jewish homeland in Palestine. The British left Palestine in 1948 and Ben Gurion declared independence and became Prime Minister, retiring in 1953. He returned as Prime Minister from 1955-63 before finally retiring from politics in 1970.

Andreas Ioannides Kalvos (1792-1869) lived in exile at the junction of Sutherland Avenue with Warrington Crescent in the first part of the nineteenth century. A Greek classical scholar, his stirring poetry fuelled the patriotic movement in the early part of the nineteenth century that led to Greek Independence from the Ottoman Empire in 1830. The inspiration for Kalvos' poetic style was a rebellion of the Greek people in 1821-29. Under Ottoman rule, Greeks were not allowed to own land. There were successful revolts against Ottoman rule by Serbs in 1804 and again in Albania in 1820. Finally in 1827 Britain proposed that Greece become an autonomous state and a naval battle at Navarino in 1827 resulted in the withdrawal of the Ottomans in 1829.

Arthur Lowe (1915-82) was a much loved stage and television character actor made famous by his role as Captain George Mainwaring in the BBC's long running TV serial of the 1970s 'Dad's Army'. He lived at 2, Maida Avenue between 1969-82. He first appeared in repertory theatre in Manchester when he was thirty. His first television appearance was in 1951. He appeared in a number of British films including 'This Sporting Life' directed by Lindsay Anderson. He was 'Swindley' in Coronation Street and was also known for his voice-overs in commercials and for children's TV programmes such as Jackanory. He was an accomplished horseman and wine connoisseur. Poignantly, he died between shows at the Alexandra Theatre, Birmingham in 1982.

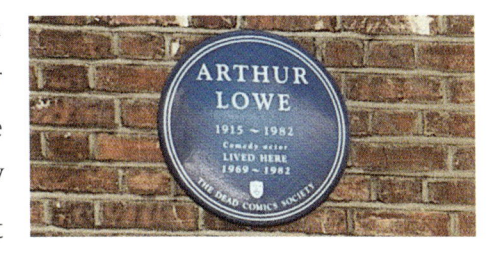

The People

Alan Mathison Turing (1912-1954) was born in London and stayed at what is now the Colonnade Hotel. He is credited with cracking the German 'Enigma' code in the Second World War from a technical centre in Bletchley, Buckinghamshire. A brilliant mathematician, Turing could also have claimed to have invented the computer. He was educated at Cambridge and Princeton universities and in 1936 published a paper called 'On Computable Numbers' introducing a calculating machine which he named the 'Turing Machine' capable of performing any mathematical calculation; a forerunner of the digital computer. He was particularly interested in artificial intelligence - the idea that a non-animal object could be made to "think".[2] In 1951 Turing was made a Fellow of the Royal Society. Sadly, he committed suicide in 1954.

Apart from the Blue Plaque residents Little Venice has played host at varying times to an array of poets, writers and influential thinkers and still does so today.

---

[2] *In this connection he published in 1952 a work on the mathematical aspects of pattern and form development in living organisms. Turing felt that artificially intelligent choices could be made based on pattern recognition, particularly in medical diagnosis.*

Poets and Writers

The poet Robert Browning (1812-1889) lived at 19, Warwick Crescent (now demolished) from 1862-87. There is a Westminster City Council green plaque commemorating Browning's time there, installed when Warwick Crescent was knocked down and rebuilt as council housing in 1966. Warwick Crescent borders the Little Venice canal pool also known as Browning's Pool. Browning was self-taught. His first poem was published in 1833, but he became known more widely with *The Pied Piper of Hamlyn*, included in *Dramatic Lyrics* published in 1842. He married Elizabeth Barrett in 1846 and moved to Florence. Elizabeth Barrett Browning, whom many contemporaries considered a finer poet than her husband, died in 1861 and Browning returned to Little Venice. Here he wrote his masterpiece: a dramatic monologue entitled *The Ring and the Book* (4 volumes, 1868-9). This poem, about a 17th century murder trial in Italy, brought Browning widespread fame. In 1878 he returned to Italy with his son, Pen. He died in Venice in 1889.

There is also a Westminster City Council green plaque in honour of Henry Hall, (1898-1989), the distinguished bandleader and impresario, at 8 Randolph Mews where he lived from 1959-1981. Henry Hall pioneered popular dance music in the 1930s and 1940s and was the conductor of a number of BBC light orchestras.

The People

Sir Stephen Harold Spender (1909-1995), poet, literary critic and editor, lived at 29, Randolph Crescent in 1933. He was an outspoken socialist in the 1930s, befriending among others the poet WH Auden who stayed at his house. Spender published *Poems* (1933) and *Vienna* (1934) in praise of socialism and the labour movement. He taught in the US, accepting the Elliston Chair of Poetry at Cincinnati University in 1953. He was knighted in 1983.

The poet John Masefield (1878-1967) was living at 30 Maida Avenue when his poem *The Everlasting Mercy* first came to public attention. He became Poet Laureate in 1930.

Ernest Dowson (1867-1900) lived at 15, Bristol Gardens during his twenties. A poet and confidante of Oscar Wilde, his best-known poetic line is: *they are not long, these days of wine and roses*.

Katherine Mansfield Beauchamp (1888-1923) was one of the great short story writers. She studied music in her early twenties at Beauchamp Lodge, 2 Warwick Crescent, then a musician's hostel but now the Centre for Counselling and Psychotherapy Education. Her stories are poetic and emotionally sensitive. Such is her writing skill that schools use her work today to show English students how to command the reader's attention at the start of a story. Here are two typical openings:

Something's happened to me -something bad. And I don't know what to do about it.
from A Bad Idea

She was just beginning to walk along a little white road with tall black trees on either side, a little road that led to nowhere, and where nobody walked at all, when a hand gripped her shoulder, shook her, slapped her ear.
from The-Child-Who-Was-Tired

Her finest works, *The Dove's Nest* (1923) and *Something Childish* (1924) were published posthumously. She died of tuberculosis, a disease for which she ardently sought a cure during the last five years of her life.

Sir John Tenniel (1820-1914) lived in Randolph Avenue (then Portsdown Road) in the 1850s. A brilliant illustrator and inventive artist, it is his original drawings that magically brought Lewis Carrol's *Alice in Wonderland* to life in 1866. He also illustrated *Alice Through the Looking Glass* in 1870.

Christopher Fry (1907-), actor, theatre director and dramatist, lived at 37 Blomfield Road in the 1950s. He first wrote a series of verse plays on religious themes, but widespread success came in both New York and London with the first performance in 1948 of his comedy play *The Lady's Not For Burning*. Fry also translated a number of French plays for the English theatre including Edmond Rostand's *Cyrano de Bergerac* (1970).

The humorist Stephen Potter (1900-1969) lived at 23, Maida Vale in the 1950s. Potter was the inventor of 'oneupmanship' through the publication in 1947 of his book *The Theory and Practice of Gamesmanship; or the Art of Winning Games Without Actually Cheating*. His playful ideas featured in a number of British film comedies of the late 1950s early 1960s, usually starring Ian Carmichael and/or Terry Thomas.

Lily Langtree, reputedly the mistress of Edward, Prince of Wales, later Edward VII, entertained in the large villa at the corner of Park Place Villas and Maida Avenue in the 1890s.

The People

Park Place
Villas

The People

The People

At various times during the twentieth century the area has allegedly been graced by Lord Alexander, Kingsley Amis, Jane Asher, Bjork, Michael Bond, Sir Richard Branson, Joan Collins, Kiki Dee, Michael Flatley, Edward Fox, Lucien Freud, Dave Gilmour, Angelica Houston, Bill Kenwright, Annie Lennox, Lulu, Sir Paul McCartney, John Mortimer, John Julius Norwich, Ben Okri, Anna Pavlova, Stephanie Powers, Ruth Rendell, Tony Robinson, Jenny Seagrove, Mel Smith, Dave Stewart, Felix Topolski, Robbie Williams and Victoria Wood. It is also whispered that one of the Eurythmics' best songs was composed in Clifton Gardens - and tomorrow, judging by the smiles on the faces of the area's estate agents, there will be many more talents arriving.

Leisure and Pleasure

Leisure and Pleasure in Little Venice

A huge variety of entertainment possibilities greet resident and visitor alike in Little Venice.

Little Venice has two theatres, two art galleries, two hotels, two churches, a garden centre and gardens, seven pubs and thirteen cafés or restaurants at the time of writing, together with a host of small shops - stocking anything from essentials for humans to inessentials for cats - and of course: the canals!

Leisure and Pleasure

Pleasure Cruises on the Canals

The best stretch for the visitor is from Camden market to Little Venice pool. The main operators are as follows:

For boat trips:

Jason's Trip	(Tel: 020 7286 3428)
London Waterbus Company	(Tel: 020 7482 2550)
Jenny Wren	(Tel: 020 7485 4433/6210)

Floating restaurants (advanced booking essential):

Lady Rose of Regents	(Tel: 020 8788 2669)
Floating Boater	(Tel: 020 7724 8740)
My Fair Lady	(Tel: 020 7485 4433)

Boats can also be chartered for private functions.

Narrow boats can be hired for more adventurous travels - ring the British Waterways Hotline on 0345 626 252.

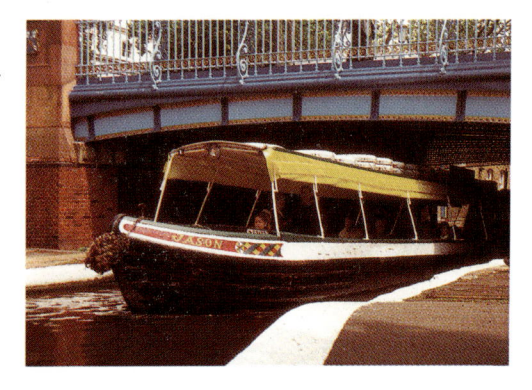

Walking Through Little Venice

Use the map in this guide to walk Little Venice - it takes about 90 minutes. You can also walk the canal path (north side) from Little Venice Pool through to Camden market, although it is advisable to avoid this path after dark. The walk takes about 40 minutes and you can take a canal boat back.

Alternatively there are guided walking tours which are fun. The best is organised at a reasonable price by The Original London Walks (Tel: 020 7624 3978). They usually start from Warwick Avenue tube station.

Theatres

Canal Café Theatre

The Canal Café Theatre at the corner of Westbourne Terrace Road and Delamere Terrace has played host to a bevy of talented actors and actresses over its twenty years. The auditorium lies above the main bar of the Bridge Inn and seats 60 at candlelit tables in an intimate and engaging atmosphere.

Leisure and Pleasure

Essentially now a Cabaret Theatre, it claims to have London's second longest running show (after Agatha Christie's *The Mousetrap*) - *Newsrevue*, still running to packed audiences. The punchy offbeat fringe comedy has produced some famous names. Rory Bremner performed there in 1984. Bill Bailey and Steve Frost have also been on stage. The content is updated every week and the cast and writing changes frequently. The show has also appeared on the Fringe at the Edinburgh Festival every year bar one since its inception. *Newsrevue* moved to the Canal Café theatre in 1984 but has also done TV specials for Channel 4 as well as innumerable clips for BBC, NBC and ITV.

The Canal Theatre offers two shows a day, seven days a week. For tickets and bookings ring 020 7289 6054.

Puppet Theatre Barge

An unexpected delight lies inside the red and yellow awning of the Puppet Theatre Barge moored alongside the Little Venice Pool. It was opened in 1982 and is operated by the Moving Stage Marionette Company. From June until October the barge hightails up the Thames to Oxford, but the theatre winters in Little Venice. The four-metre wide 'lighter' barge (hence the word lighterman to describe a worker on such boats) can seat up to 60 people in raised theatre style. Although most performances are tailored for children, a number of shows are staged each year for adults when the Puppet Theatre becomes the 'Barge Theatre'.

Inside, audiences are transported on a journey of the imagination into a magic world depicted by brilliantly manoeuvred puppets. Everything in the structure of the theatre is authentic and has a functional as well as an aesthetic appeal. Shiny brass portholes and ship's bell together with a liberal use of hardwood produce a rich effect within a working boat.

Leisure and Pleasure

The Theatre Company makes its own puppets and there is also a collection of puppets from all over the world bedecking the walls.

The company commissions plays as well as performing classical works - *Macbeth* is being staged this year for example, alongside such delights as *Three Little Pigs* and, appropriately, *Millennium Mischief*. A truly unusual and enchanting experience from masterfully manipulated marionettes. For reservations telephone 07836 202745.

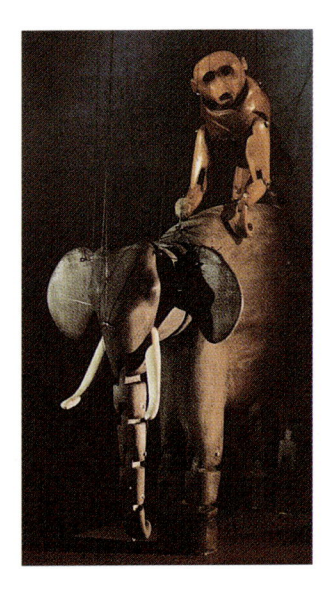

Galleries

English Watercolour Gallery

Beryl Kendall has owned this small specialist gallery at 2, Warwick Place since 1972. It specialises in the work of English watercolour artists of the nineteenth century. This period produced great artists such as Turner and Constable but others such as John Varley and David Cox are now coming into vogue and are on show here. The gallery's only concession to contemporary art is its collection of watercolours of the Little Venice area, painted by a variety of local artists featuring some of the scenes depicted in this book.

Opening Hours: Tuesday-Friday 2-6pm, Saturday 11-3.30pm
Telephone: 020 7286 9902

Cascade Art Studio

'Barge Crook', built in 1935 and one of the few remaining Regent's Canal barges, is the home of professional artist Alex Prowse, a fellow of the Pastel Society. Reputedly the first private resident in the 'Pool', having moved there in 1978, Alex has a fine reputation for canalside paintings and copper etchings.

Leisure and Pleasure

There is a permanent exhibition of his work at the Barge Crook, which has been carefully restored. The gallery room itself can also be hired out for functions and full facilities are available.

Enquiries to Jan Prowse at Barge Bloom (moored alongside), by telephone/fax on 020 7289 7050.

Hotels

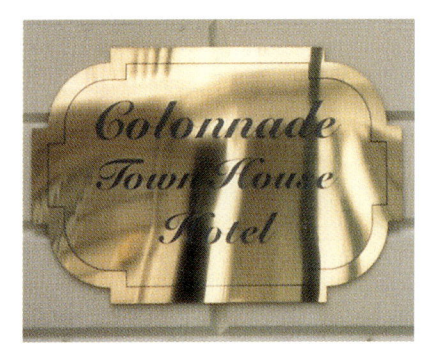

The Colonnade Town House Hotel

(formerly the Esplanade Hotel)

2, Warrington Crescent, London W9 1ER

Reservations: 020 7286 1052.

email: res_colonnade@etontownhouse.com

Worldwide reservations by UTELL

International GDS access code UI

Originally two semi-detached houses built around 1865, and for a time serving as a 'house of ill repute', the Colonnade, then known as the Esplanade, became a hospital at the turn of the century. Alan Turing, the 'Enigma' code breaker of World War II, was born there in 1912. The site became a Hotel in the 1920s. The father of psychoanalysis, Sigmund Freud, stayed there in 1938 and a suite was especially prepared in 1962 for a visit of US President John F Kennedy, now called the JFK suite. Completely refurbished in 1999, the hotel and its 43 bedrooms provide the ambience of quiet country house comfort a stone's throw from central London.

Sigmund Freud

Leisure and Pleasure

The Royal George House Hotel

30, Bristol Gardens, London W9 2JQ

Reservations: 020 7289 6146/
020 7266 2060

Roger Packham and Carol Welsford have developed a quiet retreat in the heart of Little Venice. The hotel was originally a brewery, Huggins & Co, in the late nineteenth century. The precise date when it became a hotel is shrouded in mystery, but it is named after George IV's Flagship *Royal George* and has provided overnight accommodation for weary travellers for over a century. The Bristol Mews to the rear of the hotel was formerly stables for brewery horses. Fully refurbished five years ago, the hotel offers 14 rooms with continental breakfast.

Churches

St. Saviours in Clifton Gardens at the junction with Warwick Avenue is a modern Anglican church constructed in 1976 with a dramatically tall silver spire. Previously there was a small church on the same site built in 1856 but demolished in 1972. The present building is unusual in that it is connected in its construction to residential flats.

John Pearson, the architect of Truro Cathedral, designed the Catholic Apostolic Church in Maida Avenue in 1891. It is built in the Gothic style, of which John Ruskin was the father, and was preferred to the earlier stucco of the area on the grounds that intricate brickwork was more 'honest' than less skilfully laid stone covered with stucco wash.

Catholic Apostolic Church, Maida Avenue

The Pubs

The Robert Browning, Clifton Road

Formerly called the 'Eagle'. Possesses a mahogany wood framed Victorian interior, with a number of early photographs of the area on permanent display. The first floor bar is more comfortable and serves food. There is an open seated area at the rear and wooden tables, from which passers by can be comfortably scrutinised, are always laid out in Clifton Road.

Windsor Castle, Lanark Place

Tiny homely single bar straight off Lanark Place (pedestrianised) - no food.

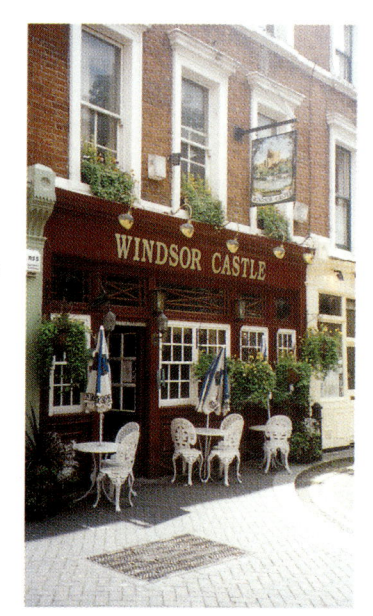

The Warrington Hotel, Randolph Avenue

Originally an old coaching inn, the current building was constructed in the 1880s. Despite being owned by the Church Commissioners it started life as a brothel but had evolved into a pub by the time of the Second World War. Wonderful sculptured exterior of shell and ionic columns with considerable designers' 'fancies' added to every corner. Original mahogany interior with cut glass inlay. There is a champagne bottle on the mantelpiece; the contents were reputedly downed by Lily Langtree at one of her legendary parties. Extensive outside lantern-heated permanent wooden seating has ensured the popularity of this splendid pub.

Leisure and Pleasure

The Warwick Castle, Warwick Place

There has probably been an inn here since the 1850s. The Warwick Castle is an attractive pub tucked away in Warwick Place away from the bustle of Warwick Avenue. In winter welcoming real fires burn in the bars, and in summer there are wooden tables outside. Food is served at lunchtime.

The Prince Alfred, Formosa Street

A true early Victorian pub built in 1862 complete with wood panelled 'snug bars' with separate double door entrances. These discrete and discreet drinking areas were designed to separate different classes of drinker - you even have to stoop to enter these tiny couched bars from within the pub itself. The pub has truly outstanding external windows of intricately designed Victorian cut glass.

The Paddington Stop, corner of Blomfield Road and Formosa Street

Modern pub serving food with extensive canalside seating which catches the sun most of the day.

The Bridge House, Westbourne Terrace Road

There has been an inn here since 1730 when the village of Westbourne was the only housing in the immediate area. The current building was constructed in the 1840s and was therefore one of the first in Little Venice. The first floor houses the Canal Café Theatre and downstairs there is a long bar with a little outside seating opposite the canal toll bridge.

Leisure and Pleasure

The Cafés/Restaurants

Maida Avenue/Edgware Road

Hsing

Sharply styled Chinese restaurant on two floors. (Reservations 020 7402 0904)

Café Laville

Stunning position on a bridge over the Maida Hill tunnel on the canal serving mainly Mediterranean snacks café style. Attractive setting with outside seating along the canal. (Reservations: 020 7706 2620)

Clifton Road

Cliftons

Basement restaurant serving an eclectic Mediterranean inspired menu. A few outside tables. (Reservations 020 7266 3786)

Raouls

A popular Mediterranean café with extensive outside seating enabling customers to watch the busy life of Clifton Road. (Reservations: 020 7289 6649)

Leisure and Pleasure

Café Rouge

Part of a chain of French inspired cafés with appropriate menus. Open until midnight, occasionally enjoying the services of an accordionist. The outside seating is in the sun for most of the day. (Reservations: 020 7286 2266)

Vicki's

Attractive café serving homemade meals and snacks. Again, the outside seating enjoys the sun for most of the day.

**Lanark Place
(off Clifton Road)**

Clifton Road

The Pizza Place

Homemade pizzas and pastas. (Reservations 020 7289 4353)

Warwick Place (between Blomfield Road and Warwick Avenue)

Green Olive

Stylish Italian restaurant on two floors next to the Warwick Castle (Reservations 020 7289 2469).

Formosa Street

Red Pepper

Trendy sister to the Green Olive, again on two floors, with a more eclectic menu. (Reservations 020 7266 2708)

Lo Spuntino

Café serving coffee and croissants and a little bit more.

Blomfield Road

Jasons

Attractive, well-established waterside fish restaurant with outside tables alongside the canal. Opposite number 60, Blomfield Road. (Reservations 020 7286 6752)

Leisure and Pleasure

Warrington Crescent

Ben's Thai Restaurant

Within the exciting architecture of the Warrington Hotel Pub but separately run on the first floor (entrance through the bar). Reputedly the first Thai restaurant within a public house in London. (Reservations 020 7266 3134)

Warwick Crescent

The Waterside Café

A barge moored in Little Venice Pool, although eating and drinking takes place on the adjacent bank. A good place to reserve boat trips, pick up a bit of canal history and relax at the poolside.

Gardens

Rembrandt Gardens alongside Warwick Avenue is a delightfully peaceful haven bordering the Little Venice Pool.

No visit to Little Venice is complete without seeing *The Lady Venice* moored at Blomfield Road. The owner has cultivated a beautiful canalside garden with pagoda, climbing wisteria and palm trees. *The Lady Venice* also supports the only 'gondola' in Little Venice, which has run aground atop the Barge and is now shelter for an exotic plant display.

Leisure and Pleasure

Each year at Whitsun holiday time certain historic private gardens in Little Venice are opened to the general public for one day. London Garden Squares Day is an initiative of English Heritage and provides the public with a rare opportunity to look behind the street façade. Details for next year's programme from LHPGT, Duck Island Cottage, St. James's Park, London SW1A 2BJ.

Clifton Nurseries in Clifton Villas, part-owned by Lord Rothschild, is a beautifully landscaped nursery and is generally considered to be central London's premier Garden Centre. The site has been a garden centre since at least 1890. Between the two World Wars the centre concentrated on supplying palms. From 1941 until 1975 Sidney Cohen ran the nursery and considerably expanded the landscaping contracting that had begun in 1950. Between 1981 and 1994 Clifton Nurseries also ran a garden antiques business which exhibited on the land opposite the British Waterways toll house office.

Leisure and Pleasure

The entrance is subtly and stylishly sandwiched between numbers 5 and 6 Clifton Villas, making the Nursery address officially 5A. There is a substantial hothouse with fabulous exotic plants and extensive displays of perennials and annuals. Many unusual plants including the rarer roses are stocked, attracting clientele from well outside London. There is also an excellent choice of large and small plant containers. Contract landscaping and garden maintenance currently at over 350 garden sites in London alone remains a substantial part of the current business.

Above:
Clifton Nurseries,
Clifton Villas

Right:
'5a' Clifton Villas

In her novel *Grasshopper* local author Ruth Rendell, writing as Barbara Vine, highlights the Nurseries' influence on the local area:

Look at that wisteria, he said, look at the garrya and its green catkins. Did I know why the gardens of Maida Vale were full of rare and beautiful plants? It was because of the Nursery in Clifton Villas, he said, the best and oldest in London, 100 years old, and it only stocked special plants. Everyone went to it to stock their gardens. Suppose, in its stead, a typical garden centre had been there, selling pampas grass and kanzans and privet. The whole place would look quite different.[3]

The nursery staff are knowledgeable and helpful, making a repeat visit an undiminished delight. Opening hours are 8.30-6.00 Monday to Saturday and 9.30-4.30 on Sunday. Telephone 020 7289 6851

---

[3] *Barbara Vine, Grasshopper, London, 2000, p.81*

Little Venice, London's best-kept secret

Few parts of London offer such a combination of romantic ambience and active entertainment as does Little Venice. Over the next five years or so there is to be further major canalside development just outside Little Venice to the south within the Paddington Basin, which will add to the attraction of the area.

For now, a stroll through Little Venice on a sunny afternoon remains an essential pleasure for resident and visitor alike. The calm of the canal offers Londoners a refreshing break from stifling offices. Visitors will be amazed and delighted by the elegance of the formal architecture, the lush abundance of soft greenery in trees and gardens and the vibrant café life nestling so close to the heart of the West End.

Little Venice, London

How to Get Here

Now that this book has whetted your appetite, you will want to come and savour the atmosphere of this unique area of London for yourself.

By Tube:

Take the Bakerloo line to Warwick Avenue

By Rail:

Paddington is the nearest mainline station. From there take a tube, bus or taxi (ask for Warwick Avenue) or walk.

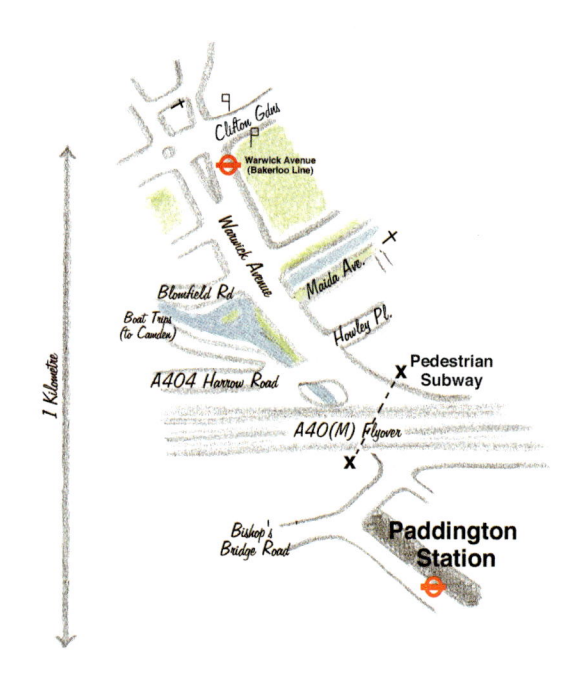

By Bus:

Numbers 6, 46, and 187 all stop in Clifton Road or Clifton Gardens

By Car:

The best road in is the A40 from the West, or Finchley Road from the North. If you are coming through the Channel Tunnel, or from the Ferry, travel through Kent and then use the Blackwall tunnel and aim for Marble Arch. Follow the Edgware Road North for one mile and turn left into Clifton Road. Parking is limited in the area on Monday to Friday but currently generally available at weekends.

By Air:

Fly to London Heathrow Airport. Take the 'Heathrow Express' train which only goes to Paddington station (Journey time 10 minutes).

Little Venice, London

Index

Adam, Robert 28
architrave 27
Arts and Craft Movement 29
Auden, W. H. 50

Bakerloo Line 82
Barge Crook 63
barge; 10, 14, 20, 23, 32, *lighter* 61
bargees 10, 14
Barrett, Elizabeth 49
Beauchamp Lodge 50
Ben Gurion, David 45
Blomfield: *Bishop* 40; *Mews* 19, 66; *Road* 10, 19, 28, 29, 31, 37, 41; *Villas* 19, 27
blue plaques 44
boat trips 14, 58
Booth, Charles: *Poverty Map* 38, 39
Bristol: *Gardens* 19, 38, 41; *Mews* 66
British Waterways 15, 32, 58, 78
Browning, Robert 17, 21, 49
Browning's Island 17
Byron, Lord 21

Cabmen's Shelter Fund 33
Camden: *market* 13,14, 58
Canal Café Theatre 59
canals: *construction* 9-15; *decline of* 16-21; *passenger trips on* 10, 13, 58
see also barges, bargees, Grand Junction Canal Company, Grand Union Canal
Cascade Art Studio 63
Catholic Apostolic Church 67
Church Commissioners 38, 39
Clarendon: *Gardens* 19, 40, 41; *Park* 40
Clark, W. S. 21
Clifton: *Gardens* 19, 37, 41, 44; *Nurseries* 31, 78; *Road* 37, 42; *Villas* 19, 27,31

Cohen, Sidney 78
Colonnade Town House Hotel 48, 64
Cookham 40

Delamere Terrace 19, 59
Dowson, Ernest 50

ecclesiastical commissioners 6
Edward, Prince of Wales 52
English Heritage 78
English Watercolour Gallery 63

Fleming, Sir Ambrose 44
floating restaurants 58
Formosa Street 19, 34, 38, 40, 42
Frederick family 6, 40
Fry, Christopher 52

George Augustus, Prince of Wales
  see Prince Regent
Giotto 28
Grand Junction Canal Company 6, 12, 17, 32
Grand Union Canal 6, 17, 32
Grasshopper 80
Great Western Railway 16, 21, 41

Hall, Henry 49
Homer, Thomas 13, 14
horses 10, 14
Howley Place 6, 18
Huggins & Co. 66

Inland Waterways Association 23
iron: *cast* 29; *railings* 28; *wrought* 29

Jessop, William 18
Junction house 32

Index

Kalvos, Andreas Ioannides 46
Kennedy, John F 65
King George IV 13, 66
King Henry VIII 6
King's Cross 10, 13

Lady Venice 77
Lanark Road 38
Langtree, Lily 52, 69
'leggers' 14, 16
Limehouse 13
Little Venice basin 10, 14, 17, 23
locks 14
London Canal Museum 13
London Garden Squares Day 78
Lord, *Thomas: Lord's Cricket* 13
        Ground
Lowe, Arthur 47

Maida: *Avenue* 6, 18, 26; *Hill* 18; *Vale* 3
Mansfield, Katherine 50
Masefield, John 50
Morehead, Sir John 40
Morris, William *see Arts and Crafts*
        Movement
Moving stage Marionette Company 61

narrow boat 10
Nash, John 13
Newsrevue 60

Paddington: *arm* 12; *basin* 12; *canal* 12, 15; *station* 21, 37
Palestine 45
Park Place Villas 6, 18, 27, 41
Pearson, John 67
pineapples 34
porticoes 28, 41
Portsdown Road 19, 40
Potter, Stephen 34, 52
Praed: *family* 40; *Street* 12, 40
Prince Regent 25
Puppet Theatre Barge 61

Randolph: *Avenue* 19, 40; *Crescent* 19; *Road* 26; *Mews* 49
'randy' 40, 43
Regency *see* Prince Regent
Regent's Canal: 17, 18, 32, 41 *Act of 1812* 13;
        Company 13; *toll house* 15
Regent's Park 13
Rembrandt Gardens 77
River Thames *see* Thames
rococo 26
Royal George House Hotel 66
Ruskin, John 21, 67

St. Saviour's 67
Shaftesbury: *7th earl of* 33
Spender, Sir Stephen 50
stucco 3, 6, 20, 25-28
Sutherland Avenue 38

'Tarporley' 10
Tenniel, Sir John 52
Thames 12, 13
Thistlethwaite, Robert 6, 40
Turing, Alan 48, 65

Venice 1, 21
Warrington: *Crescent* 40, 42
Warwick: *Avenue* 18, 19, 26, 28, 33, 40, 42; *Avenue Bridge* 15, 30, 32; *Crescent* 14, 17, 19, 40; *Jane* 40
Westminster; *city council* 49
Westbourne Terrace Road; *bridge* 15, 19, 32

Young family 40

Robert Tyler was born in London and is half-Canadian. He read history at university before branching out into a successful business career. A keen photographer, he now lives and writes in Little Venice.